The Three Ps

By Daniel Barnett

The Employment Law Library

All books in the Employment Law Library are sent for free to members of the HR Inner Circle.

1. Employee Investigations
2. GDPR for HR Professionals
3. Preventing and Defending Employee Stress Claims
4. Employment Tribunal Time Limits
5. Deconstructing TUPE
6. Changing Terms & Conditions
7. Constructive Dismissal
8. Resolving Grievances
9. HR Hazards
10. Employment Status
11. Spotting Malingering
12. Employment Tribunal Compensation
13. Hiring Staff
14. Computer and Social Media Misuse
15. Managing Sickness Absence
16. The Three Ps
17. Conflict at Work
18. SOSR Dismissals

Published by Employment Law Services Limited, Unit 3, Chequers Farm, Chequers Lane, Watford, Hertfordshire WD25 0LG

ISBN 978-1-913925-12-3

Acknowledgments

This is the sixteenth book in my series of mini-guides on employment law for HR professionals.

As always, there are people to thank. First and foremost, I'd like to thank Kathy Daniels and Fran Read for their help with the content. I'd also like to thank Tincuta Collett for the layout and design, Aaron Gaff for proofreading and Maria Rodriguez for converting the book into the formats needed for Amazon.

Most importantly, I'd like to thank the members of the HR Inner Circle for whom I primarily write these small books (and who get them all for free as part of their membership). If you're interested in learning more about HR Inner Circle membership (www.hrinnercircle.co.uk), there is more information at the back of this book.

Daniel Barnett
August 2023

ABOUT THE AUTHOR

Daniel Barnett is a leading employment law barrister practising from Outer Temple Chambers. With 25 years' experience defending public and private sector employers against employment claims, he has represented a Royal Family, several international airlines, FTSE-100 companies and various NHS Trusts and local authorities. Employee clients include David & Victoria Beckham's nanny and Paul Mason (subject of the ITV documentary 'Britain's Fattest Man').

Daniel is a past chair of the Employment Lawyers' Association's publishing committee and electronic services working party. He is the author or co-author of eight books, including the Law Society Handbook on Employment Law (currently in its 8th edition). He is the creator of the Employment Law (UK) mailing list, an email alerter bulletin service sending details of breaking news in employment law three times a week to 33,000 recipients.

Legal directories describe him as 'extremely knowledgeable and [he] can absorb pages of instructions at lightning speed', 'involved in a number of highly contentious matters', 'singled out for his work for large blue-chip companies', 'combination of in-depth legal knowledge, pragmatism, quick response times and approachability', 'inexhaustible', 'tenacious', 'knowledgeable', and 'an excellent advocate'.

He is one of the leading speakers and trainers on the employment law and HR circuit. He has presented seminars for the House of Commons, the BBC, Oxford University, HSBC, Barclays Bank, Ocado, and dozens of other organisations in-house. In 2013, 2014, 2016, and 2019 he designed — and was the sole speaker at — the Employment Law MasterClass national tour.

As well as full-time practice as a barrister and speaker, Daniel is the founder of the HR Inner Circle – a membership club for smart, ambitious HR Professionals. In 2007, he co-founded CPD Webinars Ltd, then the UK's leading webinar training company for lawyers, and sold it to Thomson Reuters in 2011.

Daniel is widely sought after as a commentator in both broadcast and print media on all legal issues. Since 2010 he has presented the Legal Hour on LBC Radio. In 2019, he launched Employment Law Matters, a weekly podcast with short explanations of employment law topics. Subscribe at www.danielbarnett.co.uk/podcast

www.danielbarnett.co.uk
Temple, London

Contents

Introduction

There are times, in any organisation, when it is necessary to tackle a difficult situation with an employee. This could be because the employee is underperforming or because they just do not fit in with the ethos and culture of the organisation. The employer may think that the best outcome would be for that employee to leave the organisation, but, for a number of reasons, it might be difficult to follow a lengthy termination process.

There is a need, therefore, for protected conversations. There are times when an employer needs to be able to have an open and frank discussion with an employee, knowing that the conversation is private and will not be discussed subsequently in a court of law.

This book covers everything the employer needs to know about protected conversations. It starts by explaining what is meant by a protected conversation and when the employer might want to enter into such a conversation. The book then looks at 'without prejudice' conversations and pre-termination conversations to clarify the difference between the two and when each should be used.

A protected conversation is likely to lead to a settlement agreement. This requires some negotiation.

It is not the purpose of this book to look at settlement agreements in detail, but it does cover the key issues that need to be considered. It also explores how to structure a discussion in order to successfully negotiate an agreement.

Having protection for the advice that a lawyer gives to an employer is also important, and therefore this book also explores the concepts of legal advice privilege and litigation privilege.

Chapter 1
What is a protected conversation and when is it relevant?

Before getting into the detail of the law, it is important to have a common understanding of what is meant by the term 'protected conversation' and when an employer might want to use such a conversation. That gives the context for everything else that is covered in this book.

A protected conversation is when the employer needs to talk to an employee but wants it to be 'off the record'. It is an opportunity to 'test the water' to see whether the employee has the same thoughts as the employer does. It could be that the employee is as unhappy with the situation as the employer, but there has never been a conversation to establish this.

It might be that the employer is concerned about raising the issue of an employee leaving the organisation and that the employee is also concerned about telling the employer that they are not enjoying their job and are planning to leave. Maybe the employer wants to 'plant the seed' in the employee's mind that they really ought to think about leaving. Maybe the employer just wants to have a conversation that is honest and open and to say that the employment relationship is simply not working out.

It is unlikely that the employer will want the conversation to be repeated in an employment tribunal or any other court of law. Therefore, there is a need for the conversation to be 'protected' if possible.

Real-life scenarios

Presume that a senior employee is underperforming. The employer wants to address this, and, to be honest, the employer's desired outcome is that the employee leaves the business. However, doing this through a series of disciplinary warnings just seems inappropriate with a senior employee. The employer does not even know whether the employee realises that they are underperforming, so there is a need to broach the subject somehow.

The risk is that the employee will accuse the employer of forcing them out of the business. If the employee has at least two years' service, there is also the risk that they will resign and claim constructive dismissal. They could argue that the employer suggesting that they might want to leave the organisation is a breach of the mutual trust and confidence that is implied into every contract of employment.

So, there is a risk in broaching the subject of the employee's underperformance. However, the employer cannot let the situation go on forever. There is a need for a protected conversation.

Alternatively, it could be that the employer and the employee are already in conflict. Maybe the employee has been accused of bullying a colleague. The employer has raised it with the employee, and the employee has retaliated by giving a long list of complaints against anyone and everyone. The employer has tried to address the employee's complaints and has also tried to address the bullying complaint against the employee. It has all become very messy, and the employer just cannot see a way forward. However, the employer knows that the best way forward does not include the option of the employee continuing to work for the organisation. Again, there is a need for a protected conversation.

The different types of protected conversation

The law recognises two different types of 'protected conversation': those that are protected under the 'without prejudice' principle and those that are protected as 'pre-termination discussions' under section 111A of the *Employment Rights Act 1996*. Each of these types of protected conversation is explored in more detail later in this book.

Chapter 2
What are the risks if a conversation is not really 'protected'?

Saying 'this is a protected conversation' is not sufficient

The employer decides that it needs a protected conversation. Is it enough to simply tell the employee that the conversation is protected? No. Just saying 'this is a protected conversation' will not give the employer any guarantee that the conversation will not be repeated in a court of law.

Of course, the employee might think that they cannot reveal the contents of the conversation. They might think that just being told the conversation is protected stops them from revealing anything. However, it does not give guaranteed protection, and the employer runs a huge risk that the employee will get good legal advice and quickly realise that the conversation is not protected.

If the employee says in an employment tribunal that the employer told them it was a 'protected conversation' and that they later realised that it was not, yes, the employer might look a bit silly, but what else does the employer risk?

The risks

By not getting this right, the employer runs the risk of losing the claim in the employment tribunal. Consider the situation of an underperforming employee. The correct and lawful way to address this is for the employer to talk to the employee about the underperformance, set targets and support and coach the employee to improve. If the employee does not improve, then the employer can give the employee a formal written warning with more targets and more support. If the employee still does not improve, the employer can give them a final written warning with more targets and more support. Finally, if the employee still does not improve, the employer can dismiss them.

For the dismissal to be fair, there needs to be a fair reason (capability would apply here) and a fair procedure. The decision to dismiss also needs to be within the range of reasonable responses. By working through this process, the employer can, potentially, achieve a fair dismissal.

However, by going straight to the final stage and saying that the employee is underperforming and needs to leave the organisation, the employer misses out all the steps of a fair procedure. So, this cannot be a fair dismissal. If the employer tries to backtrack and follow a full process, the process becomes tainted by the fact that the initial discussion showed a clear pre-judgment of the outcome. Alternatively, the conversation itself can prompt the employee to resign and claim constructive dismissal on the basis that the employer approaching them in this way breaches the implied term of mutual trust and confidence.

If the employer does not manage the protected conversation correctly, the employee can tell the employment tribunal about everything that the employer has said and done. The tribunal will soon conclude that the dismissal is unfair. Not only will the employer look a little unwise, as feared, but it will also lose the case.

Chapter 3
Getting it right –
preparatory steps

Chapter 2 illustrates the importance of getting protected conversations right. This chapter explores how to do it correctly.

Before exploring the legal aspects, there are three important areas to consider when preparing for a protected conversation. These areas are covered in more detail in Chapter 6: Negotiating Skills.

Working out what the problem is

The employer needs to define the problem. Is it underperformance? Is it a poor attitude? Does everyone in the organisation dislike the employee, meaning there are major operational difficulties? Not only does the employee deserve to know why the employer thinks there is a problem, but the employee also needs to understand the seriousness of the situation.

If the employer approaches the conversation rather timidly and says, for example, that the employee is not quite hitting targets, the employee could think that they can solve the situation with a little more effort. So, the employer needs to be clear that the situation is serious enough that it wants the employment relationship to come to an end.

Working out what to offer

What is it that the employer is offering? The employer is entering the conversation with the intention of reaching a settlement agreement. In return for the employee going quietly, the employer will need to pay an amount of money. Is this a lump sum to 'pay off' the employee? Is it an extended notice period? What is it that is being offered?

Of course, once the employee realises that they probably do need to accept that they are leaving the organisation, they are likely to want to negotiate any settlement. So, the employer needs to think about the negotiating stance. Offering all that the employer is prepared to give at the start leaves no 'wriggle room' if there is later a need to negotiate. So, the opening offer needs to be planned carefully.

Considering the desired outcome

Does the employer want the employee to leave today? Does the employer want the employee to take some time off to think about the situation and then meet again to agree the terms on which they will leave? The employer needs to plan the desired outcome, as well as a realistic fallback position (and how it will proceed if it has to opt for the fallback position).

Chapter 4
Getting it right - the legal rules

There are two types of protected conversation: a 'without prejudice' conversation and a pre-termination conversation.

Without prejudice

It is not unusual to see a document with the words 'without prejudice' written on it. This means that the document, and the content that the document is referring to, cannot be revealed in a court of law, including an employment tribunal, if the employee goes on to bring a claim at a later stage. In addition, a conversation in a difficult situation with an employee might start with someone saying that it is a 'without prejudice' conversation. Again, this means that the contents of the conversation cannot be revealed in an employment tribunal or any other court if the situation results in a claim being brought.

The reason for labelling something 'without prejudice' is to allow for a free and open conversation without either party being concerned that what they say is going to be revealed in a court at a later stage.

This purpose behind using 'without prejudice' is important. Labelling something as 'without prejudice' should not be seen as a way of doing something underhand or wrong. It is accepted that there are times when the employer and the employee just need to put their cards on the table and be open and frank with each other. However, it is also accepted that things can go wrong and can end up in a court. So, using 'without prejudice' is an enabler to solve a problem with the intention of finding a solution that works for both the employer and the employee.

If the conversation is without prejudice, the employee will not be allowed to disclose in a court any aspects of the discussion, for example, that an agreed reference was offered or the amount of money that was offered as part of a settlement.

What is required for a communication to be 'without prejudice'?

Certain requirements need to be met for a communication – written or verbal – to be without prejudice. Just as it is not enough to simply say that a conversation is protected, it is not enough to simply say that a conversation or a document is without prejudice. For the 'without prejudice' principle to apply, the document or the conversation must be a genuine attempt to settle an existing dispute.

Think of it in three steps:

Step one: There must be an existing dispute at the time that the communication takes place.

Step two: A settlement offer must be made.

Step three: The settlement must be a genuine attempt to settle the dispute.

What is really important is that the conversation, or the written communication, is a genuine attempt to settle an existing dispute. In a situation where the employer is dealing with the exit of an employee, there might be several conversations about different aspects of the situation. It is only the documents or the conversations that relate to settling the dispute that can be without prejudice.

The need for a dispute

There must be a dispute for the 'without prejudice' principle to apply. This might seem obvious, but it is an important point. If, for example, the employer wants to exit an employee, and this is the first conversation about that exit, it would be difficult to argue that the conversation is a genuine attempt to settle an existing dispute because there is no dispute. There might well be a dispute by the time the conversation ends, but the actual conversation that initially raises the concerns cannot be about a dispute; therefore, the 'without prejudice' principle cannot apply. In this situation, the employer needs to engage in a pre-termination conversation. However, if the situation then turns into a dispute, the 'without prejudice' principle might apply to later conversations.

How badly do the employer and employee have to disagree for it to be a 'dispute'? There is no requirement to be embroiled in something that has turned nasty. All that is required is for the employer and the employee to have a difference of opinion and lack of agreement. That is a dispute.

Does that mean, therefore, that if an employee raises a grievance, it is a dispute? Not necessarily, as *BNP Paribas v Mezzotero [2004] IRLR 509* illustrates.

In this case, the employee had returned from maternity leave. She raised a number of grievances, including a complaint that she had not been allowed to return to her old job. She was asked to attend a meeting with her managers, who said that the meeting would be on a 'without prejudice' basis. At the meeting, her managers suggested a termination by mutual agreement, applying the bank's redundancy scheme, which would mean a payment of approximately £100,000. They suggested that she should collect her belongings and leave, and seek legal advice.

Ms Mezzotero brought a claim to the employment tribunal, and in her evidence, she referred to the 'without prejudice' meeting. The bank argued that the meeting was subject to legal privilege (which is explored shortly) and was without prejudice, and that it therefore could not be referenced. There was a directions hearing, and the employment judge decided that it was not correct to exclude evidence of the meeting from the proceedings. The bank appealed.

The Employment Appeal Tribunal (EAT) agreed with the tribunal. Just raising a grievance did not mean that there was a dispute, and therefore, the 'without prejudice' principle did not apply. The EAT also noted that it was not realistic to conclude that everyone at the meeting had agreed to talk without prejudice, due to the unequal nature of the relationship and the vulnerability of the employee, and given that the employer only suggested that the meeting was without prejudice once it had begun.

What can be learnt from this case? Firstly, just raising a grievance does not mean that there is a dispute. If an employee raises a grievance, it means they have a concern, a complaint or something that they want to discuss with the employer. It might well develop into a dispute if the employee is not happy with the employer's response, but just raising a grievance does not immediately create a dispute.

When does something turn from being a grievance into a dispute? It is useful to think of the 'tipping point' as being when the two parties start to think about using litigation to solve the problem. At this point, the parties are saying that they are not proving able to solve the situation by having a conversation, and the situation is turning into a bigger problem – namely a dispute.

Secondly, if a meeting is without prejudice, this should be made clear at the start. It might be that a conversation will develop into a dispute. If so, there should be a pause, and it should be suggested that any further discussions are without prejudice. The employer should never start a meeting with the intention that it will be without prejudice and then land this on the employee partway through without explanation.

The communication must be a genuine attempt to settle a dispute

It is important to emphasise that the conversation or written communication must be a genuine attempt to settle a dispute for the 'without prejudice' principle to apply. If the employer offers the employee a token £1 as a way of stating that it offered a settlement, that would not be seen as a genuine attempt to settle the dispute. Again, the 'without prejudice' principle would not apply.

Note also, that the 'without prejudice' principle cannot apply where there is fraud, undue influence or some other 'unambiguous impropriety', such as blackmail or perjury. In other words, it is not possible to hide behind the 'without prejudice' principle if something improper happens.

Of course, the employer is unlikely to do something that is improper, but the employee might interpret something that the employer says or does negatively. So, as well as making sure that everyone involved in the situation acts properly, the employer also needs to think about the way that any communications might be interpreted. It is important the employer does not leave open the possibility that the employee can point to something and say that the employer acted wrongly.

In *BNP Paribas v Mezzotero* the employee argued that she had suffered direct sex discrimination and victimisation because she had raised a complaint on her return from maternity leave. If there was discrimination, then this would be unambiguous impropriety and, therefore, the 'without prejudice' principle would not apply. Put simply, if the employer misbehaves in the process of discussing the dispute, it can remove the protection of the 'without prejudice' principle.

How does an employer have a 'without prejudice' conversation?

It is very straightforward. If the employer has a verbal conversation, it can simply say that it is a 'without prejudice' conversation. The employer needs to do this at the start of the conversation. If the employee asks the employer what 'without prejudice' means, then it is important to remember that the employer is not there to give legal advice to the employee. The employer might want to give a very quick outline of what the term means, but if the employee really does not understand, then the employee should take some legal advice. The employer cannot be seen to advise the employee on what the term means and influence the employee's decision to proceed with the conversation. There is a risk that the employee might later refer to the conversation in an employment tribunal or another court, saying the conversation was not without prejudice because what the employer advised the employee was wrong, or that the employer put pressure on the employee by giving a rushed explanation and then moving ahead with the conversation.

In practical terms, this could mean that the employer does not get far into the conversation before there is a need to postpone it to allow the employee to take some advice. That can be frustrating, but it is better that the employer takes it steady and ensures that the employee fully understands rather than rushing and losing the protection of the 'without prejudice' principle.

If the employer is using the 'without prejudice' principle in written communications, then it simply needs to write this at the start of the letter or email. The employer should write 'without prejudice and subject to contract'. This means that any offer that is made is subject to both parties agreeing the terms of the agreement, as well as being without prejudice. This typically means that the employee has to agree not to proceed with a specified set of claims in return for the employer paying an amount of money.

The statement 'without prejudice and subject to contract' should be part of the heading of the communication, and never hidden away. It needs to be made very clear to the recipient that the employer intends the correspondence to be without prejudice.

Pre-termination discussions

What is really clear about 'without prejudice' discussions is that they must refer to an existing dispute. However, what happens when the employer wants to talk to an employee about exiting the organisation and there is not an existing dispute? Going back to the examples already given, this could be the underperforming senior manager who does not realise that the underperformance is causing a problem. There is no dispute because there has never been a conversation with the manager about the problem. However, the employer does not want to be in a situation where it meets with the employee and offers a settlement, only for the settlement to be disclosed subsequently in an employment tribunal because the employer was not able to label it 'without prejudice'.

This is where section 111A of the *Employment Rights Act 1996* comes in. Section 111A introduces 'pre-termination conversations'.

This has the same effect as being without prejudice. It means that the individuals concerned cannot reveal the fact or content of any communications – written or oral – relating to the situation if there is subsequently an unfair dismissal claim.

However, it is important to note that section 111A does not apply to every dispute situation. It only applies when an employee goes on to bring an unfair dismissal claim. It also applies only to 'ordinary' unfair dismissal claims. It does not apply if the employee argues that the reason for dismissal is automatically unfair. For example, the employee might argue that the reason for dismissal is because they blew the whistle, because they are a trade union member or because they raised a health and safety concern, among other reasons. In each of those situations, the protection of a pre-termination conversation would not apply.

It is worth stopping for a moment to consider this in the context of a scenario. An employer falls out with an employee who has refused a reasonable instruction to do some work in a particular way. It is not really a dispute; it is just a petty frustration, where the employee will simply not do as instructed. So, the employer arranges a pre-termination conversation with the employee to tell them it is time to end the employment relationship.

However, the employee believes that the real reason for the dismissal is that they raised a health and safety concern. They believe that the instructions they were given were dangerous, and they refused to obey for health and safety reasons. So, they argue that the proposed dismissal is automatically unfair. Although the employer has labelled the meeting as a pre-termination conversation, the employee proceeds to bring a claim of automatically unfair dismissal and therefore the protection does not apply.

So, an employer should carefully consider the sort of claim an employee might bring before embarking on a pre-termination conversation.

Section 111A only applies when the employee goes on to bring an ordinary unfair dismissal claim. So, if the employee goes on to make a different claim, such as breach of contract, wrongful dismissal, discrimination, harassment or victimisation, then the employer cannot rely on section 111A to keep the conversation confidential.

Note that there could be a rather odd situation where discussions about termination are admissible for some claims but not others. Consider this scenario: the employer has dismissed an employee and has not paid the employee the notice payment they think they were entitled to. The employee claims unfair dismissal, as well as breach of contract in relation to the unpaid notice pay.

The parties' pre-termination settlement discussions are not admissible for the unfair dismissal part of the claim, but they are for the breach of contract claim. So, the employment judge will have to listen to the evidence and then go through an Orwellian thought process to take it into account for the contract claim but ignore it for the unfair dismissal claim.

This presumes that there was no dispute at the time and, therefore, that the employer is relying on section 111A. If there was a dispute, then the employer could have labelled all of the conversations as 'without prejudice' and would potentially be able to protect them that way.

No protection if there is 'improper behaviour'

Remember that the 'without prejudice' principle does not apply if there is unambiguous impropriety. In the same way, the protection of section 111A does not apply if there is 'improper behaviour'. Acas helpfully provides the following examples of what 'improper behaviour' towards an employee might be:

- harassment, bullying and intimidation through offensive words and aggressive behaviour

- physical assault (actual or threatened) and other criminal behaviour

- victimisation

- discrimination

- putting undue pressure on a party. (This includes telling an employee before the disciplinary process has started, that if they don't agree a settlement proposal, they'll be dismissed. It also includes not giving the employee enough time to consider a proposed settlement. Acas suggests that a minimum period of 10 calendar days should be allowed to consider the proposed formal written terms of a settlement agreement, although this is not a legal requirement.)

Pre-termination discussions in practice

So, how does this work in practice? To answer this question, it is useful to look at *Faithorn Farrell Timms LLP v Bailey [2016] UKEAT/0025/16/RN*.

In this case, Ms Bailey was a secretary at a firm of surveyors. She joined in March 2009 and worked there until she resigned in February 2015. She argued that she resigned in response to her employer breaching her contract of employment and, therefore, she brought a claim of constructive dismissal.

The facts of the case were as follows. She had been working part-time. However, towards the end of 2014, her employer told her that part-time work was no longer an option. She started discussions about the possibility of her leaving the organisation and entering into a settlement agreement.

A number of pre-termination conversations took place. Bailey argued that she had started those pre-termination conversations because she felt she had no choice but to resign. She said that she was bullied and subject to sex discrimination.

A number of letters were exchanged between Bailey and her employer which were marked 'without prejudice' (by this stage, there was a dispute between the employer and Bailey, which they were attempting to settle). These letters set out each side's position with reference to a settlement and referred to pre-termination conversations that had taken place. Bailey went on to raise a grievance, saying that the employer was trying to bully her out of her role and avoid a financial settlement. She said that letters from the employer contained threats and ultimatums and that these were evidence of bullying behaviour.

She then went on to bring a claim of unfair constructive dismissal and sex discrimination in the employment tribunal. In her claim, she referred to a number of letters that had been marked 'without prejudice'. Her employer argued that she could not refer to those letters because they were without prejudice. So, before the case could proceed, the employment tribunal had to decide whether the 'without prejudice' letters were admissible and whether the fact that pre-termination conversations had taken place was, in turn, admissible.

Section 111A applies to claims of unfair dismissal (including constructive dismissal) but does not apply to other claims. Ms Bailey also brought a sex discrimination claim and, therefore, any pre-termination discussions relating to that were admissible. The tribunal also concluded that section 111A was restricted in scope and only protected the detail of any offers and conversations. It did not protect the fact that the conversations had taken place.

Ms Bailey argued that her employer had waived any privilege relating to the 'without prejudice' letters because it did not take issue with her referring to them. In addition, she said that the bullying behaviour of her employer was improper conduct and, therefore, the protection of section 111A had fallen away.

Both parties appealed to the EAT.

The EAT said that section 111A does not just cover the content of any conversations that have taken place. It also covers the fact that the discussions have taken place. Indeed, the employment judge noted that it would be commonplace in an organisation for a manager to have to report on any pre-termination conversations to a more senior manager or to HR. The judge concluded that it would defeat the purpose of section 111A if those reports to other people within the organisation were admissible. So, the EAT concluded that it is not permitted to disclose that a pre-termination conversation has taken place; it is not permitted to disclose the content of the conversations; and it is not permissible to disclose any internal communications about the conversations. However, that was only relevant to the unfair dismissal claim.

Any 'without prejudice' protection can be waived if both parties agree. However, the judge concluded that the protection under section 111A cannot be waived, even if both parties agree to do this.

The case was then remitted to the tribunal to consider Ms Bailey's argument that there had been improper behaviour due to the alleged bullying that she had experienced.

So, what can be learned from this case? It shows that neither party can reveal that a pre-termination conversation took place and that the content of the conversation is not admissible (at least, for ordinary unfair dismissal claims).

This makes a lot of sense. Imagine that in the employment tribunal, the employee says, "And then, I was called in and told that I was going to have a pre-termination conversation." Immediately, the tribunal would know that there were talks about ending the employment relationship that the employer wanted to keep private. That could be seen as affecting the way that subsequent evidence is viewed, however much the tribunal tries to ignore what has been said.

It is also a reminder of the importance of behaving properly. If there is improper behaviour, then the protection of section 111A does not apply.

The case is also a reminder that only matters relating to unfair dismissal are protected by section 111A, and it shows that this can end up being a bit messy in the employment tribunal if there are a number of different potential claims.

Chapter 5
Settlement agreements

It is not the purpose of this book to look at settlement agreements in any detail. However, it is useful to think about some of the key principles of such agreements given that the outcome of a protected conversation is likely to be a settlement agreement.

The *Acas Code of Practice on settlement agreements* (Acas Code) exists to provide guidance on the negotiation of settlement agreements and, in particular, to make sure that employers and employees understand the implications of section 111A of the *Employment Rights Act 1996* for settlement agreements.

The Acas Code makes clear that the 'without prejudice' principle means that a settlement agreement can be discussed, but with details of those discussions kept confidential and not revealed to a tribunal or a court, if there is a dispute in place. Section 111A allows for similar protection if there is not an existing dispute when the settlement agreement discussions commence.

The conditions required for a valid settlement agreement

A settlement agreement is entered into voluntarily and, in return for some form of payment, the employee waives their right to proceed with specified claims. The following conditions must be satisfied:

- The settlement agreement must be in writing.

- It must relate to a particular complaint or proceedings. (It is not sufficient to simply refer to 'full and final settlement of all claims'. The settlement agreement must specify which claims are covered.)

- The employee must have received advice from a relevant independent adviser on the terms of the proposed agreement and the impact of the agreement on the employee's ability to proceed with a complaint in the employment tribunal. (The independent adviser must be a qualified lawyer; a certified and authorised official, employee or member of an independent trade union; or a certified and authorised advice centre worker.)

- The independent adviser must have a current contract of insurance or professional indemnity insurance that covers the risk of an employee making a claim for loss as a result of the advice.

- The adviser must be identified in the agreement.

- The agreement must state that the applicable statutory conditions that regulate the settlement agreement have been satisfied.

The effect of a settlement agreement

If a settlement agreement is reached, and both the employer and the employee sign to indicate their acceptance of the terms, then the employee will not be able to proceed with any claims that are identified in the agreement. That addresses, therefore, the possibility of any discussions relating to the agreement being admitted in an employment tribunal or any other court.

For a settlement agreement to be valid, it must be entered into fairly. As already noted, there must not be any improper behaviour in the process of carrying out a pre-termination conversation. This includes putting undue pressure on an employee to agree to a settlement. Acas suggests that, as a general rule, an employee should be given a minimum period of 10 calendar days to consider the proposed terms of a settlement agreement and to seek independent advice (unless the employer and employee agree otherwise). Rushing the employee into a decision more quickly than this could be seen as improper behaviour.

Note that there is no legal right for an employee to be accompanied by a colleague or trade union representative at a meeting to discuss a settlement agreement. However, Acas recommends that it is good practice to allow this.

The role of pre-termination discussions and the 'without prejudice' principle if agreement is not reached

The protection of section 111A or the 'without prejudice' principle will become relevant if a settlement agreement is not reached. This is quite possible. It is not uncommon for an employer and employee to be unable to agree acceptable terms. In this situation, if the settlement agreement relates to an existing dispute, anything labelled as 'without prejudice' cannot be disclosed in a subsequent court hearing. If there is not an existing dispute but the route of a pre-termination conversation is used, then anything relating to a subsequent ordinary unfair dismissal claim cannot be disclosed.

Chapter 6
Negotiation skills

Agreeing a settlement agreement requires the employer to negotiate an amount of money with the employee in return for agreed terms. How should the negotiation be approached?

Understanding the different priorities of the two parties

It is useful to think about the nature of negotiations that will, hopefully, lead to a settlement agreement. The purpose is to get to an endpoint that both the employer and the employee agree on. This means there will need to be some compromise. Typically, the employer will want to reach a conclusion that involves paying as little as possible. The employee will want to reach a conclusion that involves getting as much money as possible. The two endpoints are not the same.

It is useful to remember that the employee is not necessarily being unreasonable or greedy. The employee will be genuinely concerned about the loss of income that will result from the termination of employment. The employee is likely to think about the length of time it could take to get a new job and, therefore, will want the money from the settlement agreement to cover that time. One way the employer could reduce this is by offering outplacement assistance to the employee. The more confident the employee is of getting alternative employment, the less money the employee is likely to demand.

The special nature of negotiations with employees

It is worth thinking about some specific features of the negotiations, which might be different to other commercial negotiations that the employer might be more familiar with.

- the employer has a relationship with the employee. It might be a rather fractured relationship just now, but the employer and the employee know each other, and that means that certain preconceptions and other 'baggage' are brought to the negotiations. The negotiator needs to use that to their advantage in understanding the employee but not let it cloud their judgment in determining an appropriate outcome.

- the negotiations are likely to be carried out face to face. This can be useful as 'reading' a person is always easier in a face-to-face engagement. It can also create difficulties because an emotional employee can be more difficult to manage in a face-to-face engagement.

- there is a need to reach a conclusion. In a commercial negotiation, either party can walk away if it is simply not possible to reach an agreement. In this situation, the employer has decided that the employment needs to be brought to an end, so it is not possible to simply walk away and conclude that everything will continue as it was. This does add the pressure to reach a conclusion, and the negotiator must not let this pressure rush them into reaching an agreement that is not the best for the employer.

Six steps to effective negotiation

It is useful to approach the negotiation by working through six different steps:

1. preparation

2. meeting with the employee and presenting a proposal

3. discussing the proposal with the aim of finding common ground

4. concluding the agreement

5. the employee seeking independent advice on the agreement

6. signing the agreement

1. Preparation

In many ways, it is obvious that time should be devoted to the preparation stage, but it is often rushed. This can be because the situation is causing anger, making it preferable to reach a conclusion as soon as possible. It can also be because the employer is clear about what it wants to achieve, meaning it does not take time to think about how the employee might respond.

In the preparation stage, it is important to:

- get the facts together. In the protected conversation, the negotiator will explain to the employee why it has been decided that the employment needs to come to an end. This has got to be factually correct. Setting out allegations or concerns that prove to be wrong could derail the negotiations over the settlement agreement.

- determine who is going to lead the negotiation. Ideally, more than one manager will be involved in the negotiation so that there are two people listening and thinking about responses to the employee. However, if there will be two managers, the employer should consider offering the employee the opportunity to be accompanied as well, otherwise this will look very heavy-handed.

- outline the initial terms of the settlement agreement. The negotiator needs to know the full amount that they can offer the employee and then agree a starting point.

- understand the facts about the employee. How long has the employee worked for the organisation? What other roles has the employee had? What does the employee earn? Does the employee earn additional amounts in commission and bonus and receive other payments? What skills and qualifications does the employee have (which will impact the ability of the employee to get alternative employment)? Answers to all of these questions are useful when considering the employee's likely reaction to a proposed settlement.

2. Meeting with the employee and presenting a proposal

Having completed the preparation stage, it is necessary to meet with the employee and present the proposal.

At this stage, it is important to consider how the issues will be put to the employee. Most employees will be upset when told that what they are doing is not adequate, particularly if it will lead to their employment being terminated. There is a balance to be struck between being brutally clear, so that the employee understands that this is the end of their employment, and being so destructive that the employee is devastated.

This can be partly addressed by asking questions when presenting the issues to the employee. For example, it can be useful to ask the employee to confirm the issues as they have been presented. If the employee is not able to do this or does not present the issues in the way that the employer understands them, this suggests that the presentation of the issues has not been sufficiently clear and needs to be revisited.

Taking a break if the conversation becomes very emotional is a useful tactic. It is useful to pepper the meeting with adjournments to give both parties a break from what will almost certainly be a very intense discussion. The breaks can allow the parties to calm down and think about what is being said.

3. Discussing the proposal with the aim of finding common ground

Once the employer has presented the issues and a proposed settlement, the employer and the employee will need to agree terms. Sometimes, this is a surprisingly smooth process, particularly if the offer is generous. However, it will often involve some negotiation, so it is important to establish areas of common ground first.

Doing this can save a lot of energy if there are things the employer and the employee can agree on. For example, in a settlement agreement, there might be a proposal that involves:

- an amount of money

- payment terms (which could be to pay all the money on a certain date or to pay the money in set instalments over a period of time)

- terms relating to the employee's notice, which could be a payment in lieu of notice, a period of garden leave or even an agreement that the employee will work part of the notice (although this will probably be unlikely in this sort of situation)

- an agreed reference

- an agreement that the settlement will not be discussed with anyone

- an agreement about which external bodies, such as customers or clients that the employee dealt with, will be told about the reason that the employee has left the organisation

A common mistake is to put all the focus on the money and presume it is what the employee will want to discuss. Some of the other issues, particularly what people will be told about the exit, can be very important to the employee.

The employer needs to think outside the box in terms of what will be offered. Different employees will have different priorities. For some, an offer to continue insured benefits for a period may be important. Others may want to retain company equipment (for example, a mobile phone and laptop) that they have been using for work. Some employees may want payments to be made into their pension. For others, knowing that a reference will be provided to new employers might be a key issue. It is important for the employer to take the time to consider what they know about the employee and what makes them tick before they put an offer on the table.

It is also important for the employer to appreciate the parameters within which the offer is made – what is the employer's risk if the employee does not accept the offer? Notice pay and accrued but untaken holiday pay will be payable (and taxable) as an absolute minimum. Any consideration above this needs to look at the different risk areas. The basic award for unfair dismissal follows statutory redundancy calculations and can be calculated at www.gov.uk/calculate-your-redundancy-pay. This would be payable as an absolute minimum if an unfair dismissal finding were made.

Compensation for ordinary unfair dismissal is thereafter linked to loss of earnings flowing from dismissal. If the employer is paying in lieu of notice, then it should give consideration to the fact that these 'losses' will not begin to flow until the pay-in-lieu period has expired. The employer should then think realistically about how long it is likely to take the employee to secure an alternative position and whether there is likely to be a disparity between their current pay and their pay in a new job. This gives the employer a ballpark monthly loss figure to work from. The employer should be sensible but not stingy and leave itself wriggle room to negotiate. Compensation under a settlement agreement is tax free up to £30,000 (whereas pay in any new job, or indeed in the employee's old job, is received net). Offering a month's gross pay as an offer of settlement is worth more in the employee's pocket than if they had actually worked that month. The employer should also consider how it might benefit: there will be no need to go through an open process of dismissal with the drain on resources that will entail, no risk of a costly tribunal claim and the ability to move the business forward without delay.

4. Concluding the agreement

Settlement agreement discussions can go on indefinitely. There comes a point at which the employer needs to draw the conversations to an end and make a final offer.

There is a skill in determining when it is appropriate to make a final offer and state that there is nothing more to negotiate. If the negotiator states that an offer is final, the employee refuses to agree to it and then the negotiator goes back with a 'final, final offer', then credibility is lost.

In deciding when to call an end to the discussions, it is important to think about the implication of walking away from the discussions without an agreement.

If there was a pre-existing dispute and the discussions have been labelled 'without prejudice', then, assuming that there has been no 'unambiguous impropriety', nothing will be admissible. Likewise, if the discussion was raised as a protected conversation relying on section 111A of the *Employment Rights Act 1996*, then the fact of the discussions and their content will also, so long as there has been no 'improper behaviour', be inadmissible in relation to any ordinary unfair dismissal claim.

By bringing negotiations to a close and ending the employment without agreement, the employer may actually call the employee's bluff. The employer will face the risk of an unfair dismissal claim, but the employee will face loss of income and need to obtain new employment. This may well focus the employee's mind such that a re-statement of the offer after employment has ended (either on a 'without prejudice' basis or using Acas) may be met with a more positive response. Indeed, before the employee is able to make a claim to the employment tribunal, they will be required (with some limited exceptions) to engage with Acas Early Conciliation. This will offer a further opportunity to settle, and it might be more successful than face-to-face negotiations. If early conciliation fails and the employee subsequently makes a claim to the employment tribunal, Acas has a statutory duty to try to facilitate settlement of the claim. So, all is not lost if it is not possible to reach an agreement at this stage.

5. The employee seeking independent advice on the agreement

If the settlement talks go well and the employee is satisfied with the offer, they are legally required to seek advice on the agreement before they sign it. There is no legal requirement for the employer to pay for this advice, though it is common for the employer to offer, usually with a limit on the amount the employee can spend.

The advice the employee receives must come from an independent adviser, and therefore the employer's company solicitor cannot be used for this purpose.

After receiving independent advice, the employee may want to reconsider some of the clauses in the settlement agreement, which can be frustrating for the employer. However, this is the right of the employee, and the employer should be prepared for this eventuality.

If the employee asks for some aspects of the agreement to be reconsidered, it is useful for the employer to ask the employee to share their concerns. Is the employee genuinely concerned? Do they really want the points to be revisited, or are they concerns raised by the independent adviser that the employee does not share? This does not mean that the points just go away, but it could mean that the employee could go back to the adviser and state that they are happy for the points to stand.

6. Signing the agreement

The final step is for the agreement to be signed. The independent adviser will have explained to the employee what this means, specifically that the employee will not be able to progress with certain claims once the agreement has been signed and the employer has done whatever is set out in the agreement.

Chapter 7
Additional resources

Employers should now have a clear understanding of the different legal rules surrounding protected conversations. There is a handy flowchart at Appendix 1 to help Employers work out whether a planned conversation with an employee could be protected and, if so, on what basis.

There are also some scenarios at Appendix 2 that explore how without prejudice and pre-termination conversations might come into play in real life.

It is not possible to provide scripts or letters that give a verbatim plan of what should be said whenever an employer wants to hold a pre-termination conversation with an employee. Each situation is specific to its own facts. However, Appendix 3 contains a template script and letter that outline what an employer might want to cover in a conversation with an employee.

Chapter 8
Legal privilege

Beyond the protection of conversations between the employer and the employee, there is another area of protection that should be considered – that of communications between a client and the client's lawyer.

Assume that an employer is thinking of restructuring its business and, as part of that process, wants to terminate the employment of a number of senior managers who have not been performing well. The employer wants to understand the legal ramifications of doing this, so it contacts a lawyer to ask for advice. The employer would not want that advice to then be disclosed if one of the senior managers brought a claim in the employment tribunal. The advice would reveal that the employer had planned what was going to happen before any consultation had taken place, and that could lead to a conclusion that the dismissals were procedurally unfair.

A lawyer's client wants to be able to seek legal advice without the worry that the advice will be made public at a later stage. This is covered by 'privilege'. There are two main types of privilege.

Firstly, there is legal advice privilege. This is the protection of confidential communication, and evidence of communication, between a lawyer and their client.

Secondly, there is litigation privilege. This is the protection of confidential communication, and evidence of communication in relation to litigation, between a lawyer, their client and a third party, or between a client and a third party.

Legal advice privilege

Legal advice privilege applies to the advice given by a lawyer to their client. As well as solicitors, barristers and legal executives working in private practice, it covers in-house company lawyers advising their company or union lawyers advising an employee.

It does not apply to advice given by someone who is not a lawyer. For example, if an accountant gave legal advice on a matter, this would not be covered by legal advice privilege.

The privilege only applies to legal matters. An in-house lawyer often has a dual role of advising on legal and commercial matters. The advice on legal matters will be covered under privilege, but the advice on commercial matters will not. For the legal advice to be protected, it must be the dominant purpose of the communication. It is not enough for it to be a purpose – it must be the dominant purpose.

Privilege only applies to the advice given to a client. The definition of a client is rather narrow and only covers individuals who are authorised to give instructions to a lawyer and receive advice from a lawyer about the matter under discussion. This means, therefore, that wider communication with a range of managers about a particular issue will not be covered by legal privilege if they are not the ones who are giving instructions to the lawyer.

This is a really important point, particularly when thinking about the circulation of advice from a lawyer. If documents are circulated outside the client team, then the privilege relating to those documents is likely to be lost.

A 'client' does not have to be one person. There can be a client team. Whether the client is one person or a team needs to be clearly defined, both to the lawyer and to all those within the organisation who are involved in the situation.

The privilege applies to communications. This can include oral communication and written documents. If the client prepares documents and these documents are not communicated to the lawyer, they are not privileged. However, any preparatory material from the lawyer is privileged. The employer should work on the basis that any material that the lawyer produces that can only be produced because of the relationship with the client will be privileged even if the material is not sent to the client.

What does this mean in practice?

Firstly, it means that the employer must start by clearly defining the client or the client team. There will often be a number of people on the periphery of an issue who want to know what is going on. Any persons defined as the client must be clear on what they can and cannot do in terms of receiving and passing on any communications about the issues. It must be made clear that people on the periphery cannot contact the lawyer directly for clarification. They must go to those who are defined as the client or the client team and ask them to seek the required advice.

The employer also needs to clearly define the client or the client team to the lawyer. The lawyer should be asked not to engage in any discussions with anyone in the organisation who is not part of this client definition.

Secondly, it means that the employer needs to think carefully about the advice it requires. If the employer needs a mix of legal and commercial advice, these lines of communication should be separated. Communications about the legal matters will be privileged, but any advice about the commercial aspects will not. Therefore, questions and communications might need to be carefully framed.

Thirdly, the employer must think about the way that information is circulated. Once it has been circulated outside the client team, it is likely to lose privilege. As with any sensitive communication, it should only be provided on a need-to-know basis.

Some other useful tips

Regarding legal privilege, in addition to the actions outlined above, an employer should:

- engage a lawyer sooner rather than later. This avoids the creation of a lot of unprivileged documents because anything written down that is not legal advice is not privileged.

- take direction from the lawyer once they are engaged. For example, do not start investigating an issue or interviewing employees without confirmation from the lawyer that this is appropriate. Again, if it is not legal advice, then it is covered by legal privilege.

- keep privileged and non-privileged documents separate so that there is clarity for all involved. Consider whether it would be useful to password-protect privileged documents.

- avoid annotating documents produced by a lawyer and make others aware that they should also avoid doing this. Doing so could mean that the documents lose their privilege because they are no longer advice that is specifically from a lawyer.

- put a confidentiality agreement in place if privileged material needs to be discussed with a third party. It can also be useful to limit discussions to meetings or telephone conversations rather than creating lots of additional documents.

- if there is a broader issue that requires both legal and commercial advice, keep the issues separate, both in documentation and in discussions. For example, this could mean separating the two issues out in a board meeting, with one set of minutes for the commercial issues and a separate set of minutes for the legal issues.

- be clear about what the roles and responsibilities of the client are, and make clear that those who are not the 'client' should not take on these roles and responsibilities. Such roles and responsibilities could include preparing briefing notes, writing letters of instruction and writing letters asking for clarification on specific points.

Most importantly, remember that if something isn't written down, it can't be a disclosable document – meaning the employer doesn't have to disclose it during litigation. Note, though, that the employer must always be truthful about any non-privileged verbal conversations when giving evidence.

Litigation privilege

Litigation privilege covers communications (both oral and written) between a client, the client's lawyer and third parties that have been created once litigation is contemplated or has commenced if the main purpose of the communications is for use in litigation.

Unlike legal privilege, litigation privilege includes communications that have been provided by non-legal advisers. So, for example, advice prepared by an accountant can be covered by litigation privilege.

Firstly, there must be litigation (which includes arbitration). It must be contemplated (but more than just a vague possibility or risk) or underway.

Secondly, the documents covered by litigation privilege must be created for the main purpose of obtaining information or giving advice related to the contemplated litigation. The 'main purpose' is important here.

For example, presume that an employee has been dismissed for revealing confidential information. The organisation might want to learn from the situation and understand how measures can be put in place to stop it from happening again in future. The main purpose of a report written to address this would not be to address any litigation. As a result, litigation privilege would not apply to the report.

Also, consider what might be meant by a 'third party'. This could be, for example, an insurer or a group company. Any material shared with such parties would still be privileged as long as there is a clear and limited purpose for the sharing. Care needs to be taken here. Information should only be shared if the third party needs to know it.

Some practical tips

There are some practical points to consider when managing privileged material. If these are not addressed, then privilege can be lost.

The material should not be circulated more widely than is necessary. The client should always think about the reason for sending the material to other people. If there is not a good reason to do so, the material should not be circulated.

If material is circulated, it should ideally be marked as 'confidential and privileged' (that is not a legal requirement, but it helps demonstrate the restricted circulation). Just labelling the information as confidential and privileged will not mean that it is, but it reminds individuals that they are dealing with very sensitive information. It should be made clear to the recipients that it should not be circulated onwards. If someone thinks it is necessary for an additional person to see the material, they should agree this with the client before circulating.

It is also important to think about any accompanying emails or letters that give a commentary on advice given by a lawyer. For example, this could be forwarding a letter of advice from a lawyer to a wider group of people and writing an accompanying email that summarises what the letter of advice says. The letter itself might be privileged, but the commentary might not be. If the commentary is detailed, then the protection of the advice from the lawyer is of minimal benefit.

And, very importantly, it is useful to discourage the sharing of material by email. People forward emails much more readily than written communications, and it is easy to lose control if email is the main method of communication.

Chapter 9
Summary

This book covers the different ways of holding protected conversations with employees and the different ways in which communications with lawyers and/or other third parties can be protected from disclosure. In summary:

- where an employer is in dispute with an employee, the employer is generally able to rely on the 'without prejudice' principle to protect the content of any negotiations aimed at resolving that dispute from disclosure in resulting legal proceedings.

- where there is no dispute and the employer's aim is to remove the employee from employment, the employer can protect the fact and content of discussions from disclosure in any flowing ordinary unfair dismissal claim by relying on the protection set out in section 111A of the *Employment Rights Act 1996*.

- the employer needs to make clear to the employee that it is either relying on the 'without prejudice' principle or holding a 'pre-termination conversation' before holding any discussion.

- any settlement reached is likely to need to be incorporated into a settlement agreement upon which the employee will need to take independent legal advice.

- legal advice privilege can be relied upon to protect advice received from a solicitor from disclosure.

- litigation privilege can be relied upon to protect documentation and correspondence with lawyers and third parties if it is created for the main purpose of obtaining information or giving advice related to issued or contemplated litigation.

Appendix 1

Without Prejudice and Protected Conversations Flowchart

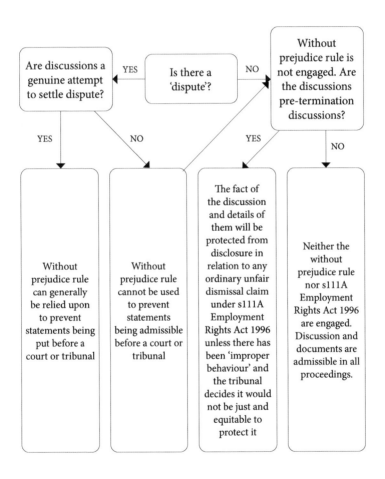

Are discussions a genuine attempt to settle dispute?

YES →

Is there a 'dispute'?

NO →

Without prejudice rule is not engaged. Are the discussions pre-termination discussions?

YES

NO

YES

NO

Without prejudice rule can generally be relied upon to prevent statements being put before a court or tribunal

Without prejudice rule cannot be used to prevent statements being admissible before a court or tribunal

The fact of the discussion and details of them will be protected from disclosure in relation to any ordinary unfair dismissal claim under s111A Employment Rights Act 1996 unless there has been 'improper behaviour' and the tribunal decides it would not be just and equitable to protect it

Neither the without prejudice rule nor s111A Employment Rights Act 1996 are engaged. Discussion and documents are admissible in all proceedings.

SEE NOTES >

There will generally be an existing **dispute** where an employee has brought a claim or might reasonably contemplate bringing a claim

In order to be regarded as a **'genuine attempt to settle'** the dispute the parties must do more than simply set out their differing positions

Even if the **without prejudice** rule is engaged it **cannot be relied upon if**:

- The question is whether a concluded settlement was reached in a dispute

- There is evidence of misrepresentation, fraud or undue influence

- There is evidence of perjury, blackmail or other procedural impropriety

Pre-termination discussions are any offer made or discussions held, before the termination of the employment in question, with a view to it being terminated on terms agreed between the employer and the employee (s111A(2) ERA 1996)

The ACAS Code on Settlement Agreements lists examples of **Improper behaviour** to include:

- All forms of bullying, harassment, and intimidation

- Physical assault or the threat of physical assault or criminal behaviour

- All forms of victimisation

- All forms of discrimination

- Putting undue pressure on a party

Appendix 2
Sample script and letter

Sample script for a pre-termination conversation

Thank you for coming to this meeting today. I have asked you to attend the meeting because I have concerns about your ongoing employment in the organisation. Therefore, this is a meeting that is referred to as a pre-termination conversation. It is allowed for in law, and is an opportunity for me, as the employer, to discuss my concerns with you with the aim of ultimately agreeing a settlement agreement that will set out terms on which you will leave the organisation.

As this is a pre-termination conversation it is a discussion that neither of us will subsequently be allowed to refer to in a court of law, should this matter end up in litigation.

I do understand that this might come as a shock to you. Before I detail my concerns about your ongoing employment, I would like to pause to ask if you have any initial questions about the procedure and about the way that this meeting is being conducted.

[Pause and allow the employee to ask any questions. Continue when any questions have been addressed.]

As I have noted, I do have specific concerns about your ongoing employment in the organisation. Specifically, these concerns are *[specify the nature of the concerns. Be clear and precise, and give examples. Avoid talking generally about 'poor performance' or 'attitude that is unhelpful'. The employee needs to understand the nature of the problem.]*

Do you have any comments or questions about these concerns?

[Pause and allow the employee to ask questions or argue their side of the story. If the employee raises new issues that you were not aware of, it might be necessary for you to adjourn the meeting at this point so that you can investigate the issues raised. If there is nothing raised that requires you to adjourn, proceed with the next section of this script.]

Thank you for your comments. You have raised some points that are clearly important to you. But they do not change the situation as I see it. For the reasons that I have already given [repeat the key points from the reasons here], it is not feasible for you to continue working in this organisation.

For that reason, I would like to discuss the terms of a settlement agreement with you. I fully appreciate that you will need time to think about the terms that I set out for you. In addition, you are legally required to receive advice from an independent adviser. It is not my intention, therefore, to finalise a settlement agreement today. However, I do want to explain the proposed terms to you so that you can go and think about them, and then we can arrange to meet again to discuss the terms further.

The proposed terms are [set out the proposed terms. You might not want to set out your final position here, allowing yourself some room to negotiate. Be clear about any terms – for example, you might offer an amount of money that will be paid in instalments or, if you offer an agreed reference, you might put some caveats on this, such as not referencing some specific events.]

As I have said, it is not my intention to try to conclude a settlement agreement today. I would like you to go away and think about what I have said and then come back to me with your thoughts and any questions that you might have.

If we agree terms that we are both happy with, you will need to take advice from an independent adviser. We can discuss the process of doing this in more detail when we next meet.

[NOTE - this is unusual but can be done if there is a compelling reason to keep the employee away from the workplace: Until our next meeting, there's no need for you to come into work; we won't ask you to do any work, but we'll continue paying you as normal. Please don't contact any of our clients or customers, and please

don't discuss this conversation with any of your work colleagues.]

For today, I would like to suggest that we now bring the meeting to an end, unless you have any specific questions. **[Pause to allow the employee to ask questions and you to answer them.]**

We will need to meet again; let's meet again on **[agree a date, time and place].**

Before we close the meeting, I would like to emphasise that the meeting we have had today is a pre-termination conversation. This means that if the issues we have discussed are subsequently raised in a court of law, the fact that the meeting has taken place, and the matters discussed in the meeting, cannot be disclosed.

Letter to an employee following a pre-termination conversation

*Dear [**name of employee**]*

*I am writing to confirm the contents of the meeting that took place on [**date**]. Present at the meeting were [**list all the people who were present, giving their names and job titles**].*

As I explained to you, the meeting that we had today was a pre-termination conversation. This is allowed under section 111A of the Employment Rights Act 1996, and it means that the fact that the meeting took place and the content of the meeting cannot be disclosed in a court of law should we subsequently end up in a dispute relating to the matters that we discussed that involves litigation.

*At the meeting, I explained to you that concerns have arisen, meaning that your ongoing employment with the organisation is untenable. [**Detail the issues.**]*

*As I explained, this means that your employment will be terminated. I want to agree a settlement agreement with you, and I outlined to you the proposed terms of that agreement. They are [**detail what was offered as a settlement agreement**].*

I also explained to you that you cannot sign the settlement agreement until you have received advice from an independent adviser. That adviser must be a qualified lawyer; a certified and authorised official, employee or member of an independent trade union; or a certified and authorised advice centre worker. The organisation is prepared to pay for the cost of this advice up to a maximum amount of £[amount]. You must provide an invoice, and then I will arrange payment.

However, before we get to the stage of agreeing a settlement agreement, I have asked you to take some time to think about today's conversation. We have agreed to meet again at [time] on [date] at [place] to continue our discussion.

Once we have agreed the terms of the settlement agreement, you will be given a period of 10 calendar days to reflect on those terms before you are asked to sign the agreement.

If you have any questions before we next meet, please do not hesitate to contact me.

[NOTE - this is unusual: We have agreed that you will not attend work during the period between now and when we next meet. Please note that this means you should not make any contact with company clients or customers. If you are in contact with any fellow employees, you should only discuss the matters raised at today's meeting with the colleague or trade union representative accompanying you to the meetings with me.]

I do appreciate that this is a difficult situation for you, so please do let me know if there is any specific support I might be able to arrange for you.

Yours sincerely

[Name and job title]

.

Appendix 3
Scenarios

Scenario 1

A senior employee is underperforming. The employer wants the employee to leave the business, but it does not want to go through a series of performance warnings. The employer does not know whether the employee even realises that they are underperforming, so it needs to broach the subject somehow.

Planning the process is critical. There are all sorts of risks to consider, and – particularly with senior employees – the employer might encounter a situation where other senior employees, or even members of the board, are discussing the underperformance and the plans or hopes to get rid of the employee. This is where the employer needs to warn the senior employees and board members that their conversations – and especially their emails – aren't privileged and will likely be disclosable if anything goes wrong. How can the employer gain the protection of privilege? It must either take legal advice on the specific issue so that documentation going via the solicitor is potentially covered by legal advice privilege or assess whether litigation privilege might apply, although, in reality, if the situation has never been addressed with the employee before, then how can there be a real risk of litigation?

There is a risk in broaching the subject of the employee's underperformance, just as there is a risk in not doing so. There could be a poor reaction; a denial of what the employer are suggesting; or a counter-attack, blaming others or other circumstances for the underperformance that is alleged. There could even be an allegation that the employer is discriminating against the individual, perhaps on grounds of their age given their seniority. What if the employee accuses the employer of "forcing them out of the business"? What if they say, "I've had this health condition for years and so-and-so has always known about it"?

The employer should not forget some of the basic skills of managing a protected conversation correctly. It needs to work out what it wants to say: what's the problem, what's the employer's suggested solution and what outcome does it want to achieve?

Firstly, what is the problem? Is it underperformance? Is it a poor attitude? Does everyone in the organisation hate the employee and that is causing major operational difficulties? The employer needs to define the problem. Not only does the employee deserve to know why the employer thinks there is a problem but they also need to understand the seriousness of the situation. If the employer approaches the conversation and rather timidly says that the employee is not quite hitting targets, the employee could think that they can solve the situation with a little more effort. No. The employer only going through the process of a pre-termination discussion because it wants the employment relationship to come to an end. So, the employer needs to be clear that it is talking about a serious situation – not something minor or trivial that can be quickly addressed.

Secondly, what is the employer offering? The employer is going to start the conversation with the intention of reaching a settlement agreement. In return for the employee going quietly, the employer needs to pay an amount of money. What is that amount going to be and what room for negotiation does the employer have? The employer needs to think about its negotiating stance and the organisation's desire to get things done. Generally, the more there is a need for a quick resolution, the more attractive the offer to the employee will need to be. The employer offering all that it is prepared to give at the start leaves no 'wriggle room' if negotiation is needed later, so it will be necessary to think carefully about the opening offer.

Thirdly, what outcome does the employer want to achieve? Bear in mind that the Acas Code recommends that an employee is given ten days to consider an offer from the point at which they receive it in writing. If the employer wants the employee to leave sooner, is it comfortable taking the risk that the employee will argue that they've had insufficient time? Does the employer want the employee to take some time off to think about the situation and then meet again to agree the terms on which they will leave? They're not entitled to the time off, but it might help. The employer should think about its desired outcome, as well as a realistic fallback position (and how it will proceed if the fallback position is needed).

Once the employer is armed with a plan, the conversation can take place. The employer should explain to the employee that it wishes to speak with the employee on a 'without prejudice' basis and that it would like to have a pre-termination conversation in line with section 111A of the Employment Rights Act. That makes the position clear and underlines the purpose of the meeting. There is arguably no 'dispute' at the start of the meeting, so the 'without prejudice' principle may not initially apply. This is why it is important to make reference to this being a pre-termination discussion (as no dispute is required for this form of protection to apply). The employer should have some examples ready to open the discussion, if needed, and then explain that there are issues that need to be addressed but that the hope is that a solution can be reached that is acceptable to all. The employer should always be prepared to pause a meeting to allow for emotions to calm and objectivity to be restored.

H2: Scenario 2

Consider another scenario: misconduct that can't quite be proved. It's quite a common situation. It could be the sometimes-too-robust manager, the employee with an attitude, the employee who doesn't quite pull their weight or the two employees who just can't get along. Employers likely come across them and know that the amount of time, energy and resources these employees take up is disproportionately high when compared to all the other jobs on their desks. But without sound evidence to support a conclusion that employment can be fairly terminated, there's always going to be the risk of a claim, which will just take up more time and energy and bring with it the risk of losing too.

In this type of situation, complaints or other documentary evidence may already exist, either because the parties are in the middle of a disciplinary or performance management process anyway or because there is a general level of dissatisfaction with the employee concerned. Those types of documents probably won't attract any protection under any form of legal privilege, but the employer should consider whether they might assist as part of the protected conversation or whether they might make things worse. If the employer has already taken legal advice, that will be privileged. But the employer should be wary of referring to the advice in such a way that it might be seen to have waived privilege.

Just as with the underperforming manager in scenario 1, starting these conversations is often the hardest part, so careful planning is important. A discussion with the employee about how they view their employment at the company can often be productive. It may reveal concerns, grievances or general unhappiness with the workplace that allow the employer to suggest a settlement agreement as a possible solution. Even if the employee rejects all allegations and insists that they're happy at the company and a delightful employee, the employer has opened the door on that conversation and can then move on to either put various allegations to the employee or simply say that the company takes a different view and has decided to have a serious conversation about the future.

In both cases, the employer should be prepared to confirm the proposed settlement in writing. The employer needs to be able to produce a settlement agreement at some point anyway, but, if necessary, that can be done at a later stage when terms have been broadly agreed. If the employee is interested in principle or just wants to understand their options, their adviser will want to know what precisely the employer is offering. Unlike a disciplinary or appeal decision, there's nothing inappropriate about having a letter ready to hand over, as long as it clearly states that the offer is made in accordance with section 111A, is 'without prejudice and subject to contract' and may be rejected without the threat of immediate consequences. Preparing a proposal in writing before the conversation takes place also allows the employer to make sure it's covered all the essential points: notice pay, holidays, bonuses and benefits, and the all-important ex gratia offer. The employer being calm and organised in its approach will likely result in a calm response from the employee and their adviser.

Also by
Daniel Barnett

Available on Amazon
or visit
go.danielbarnett.com/books

JOIN DANIEL EVERY SATURDAY EVENING AT 9PM WHEN HE PRESENTS THE ALL-NEW

LBC LEGAL HOUR

— OR CATCH UP VIA THE GLOBAL PLAYER, **AT** bit.ly/lbclegalhour

SATURDAYS, 9PM

Dear HR Professional,

I take my hat off to you.

Having supported the HR community for so many years, I know It's a challenging job you do, sometimes under really difficult circumstances.

The tricky HR issues you have to handle must take up a tremendous amount of your time, your energy and your brain power. I bet it can be exhausting for you to work under that level of pressure.

Being An HR Professional In Today's Business Environment Is TOUGH!

Maintaining your high standards of professionalism must be a real struggle, especially when your efforts and expertise often go unappreciated.

I'll wager you have to make decisions on challenging HR situations you've sometimes never encountered before. Even if you're part of a team, it must sometimes feel like you're working in isolation.

With so much complexity and ambiguity, do you ever find you're not clear whether you're doing the right thing when there's so much to think about?

I expect it can be draining too. You've got to make tough decisions which may be unpopular.

The pressure's on you to ensure people are treated fairly while the business complies with its legal obligations.

It's a thankless task, especially if you've got grief coming at you from all sides.

Doubt can creep in too. Even though you're an extremely competent professional, you might even begin to question yourself... What if you've got it wrong?

You've got to cope with all that, whilst constantly having to convince any doubting stakeholders you're adding value to the business.

That pressure must take its toll on you.

You wouldn't be human if it didn't cause you tension, stress or even worse!

Being the caring professional you are, I bet you often take work home with you.

If You're Not Careful The Stress WILL Creep Up On You

And I don't just mean opening your laptop on your couch when everyone else is watching Eastenders.

We all know of families and relationships that come a poor second to the pressures and challenges faced at work.

Yours too..?

But does it have to be that way?

Should you feel the responsibility of the HR world is entirely on your shoulders and that you've got to bear that burden alone?

The answer is a firm no.

It doesn't have to be like that.

There Is An Answer To Help Make Your Work & Your Life Much Easier For You

There's a place you can get all the help, support, advice and encouragement you need to ease the constant pressure you have to bear.

> ### It's called the HR Inner Circle.

It will lift the burden you're carrying by giving you swift access to comprehensive resources and live practical guidance you can implement right away.

It's information I know will save you time, energy and effort.

It's a vibrant, active community of caring, like minded HR professionals willing to help you.

There are resources packed full of practical, actionable advice for you that's difficult to find anywhere else.

And it doesn't matter what you're working on.

Whether it be workforce engagement, attracting and keeping talent, diversity and inclusion or employee health and well being, you'll find support for all of that.

You're covered even if you're working on one of those tricky, sensitive, people problems you never see coming until they land squarely on your plate.

Timely Support To Make Your Job Easier, Can Be Rapidly Found In The HR Inner Circle

As a member of the HR Inner Circle, to get the support you want…

…just ask.

Your first port of call is the vibrant Facebook group, bursting at the seams with incredible HR professionals like you.

Just post your question and let it bubble and simmer in the collective genius of the group.

By the end of the day, you'll have at least 3-5 comments on your post, often more.

You'll get relevant, insightful and practical guidance that comes from the hard earned experience of your fellow members.

Often you'll get a response within a couple of hours. Sometimes you'll get an answer within minutes - even if it's late in the evening!

This highly active community never fails to astound me with just how willing they are to help fellow HR professionals like you.

They readily and generously share their hard earned knowledge and experience.

You Can Get Answers From Real People Quickly AND From Our Extensive Resource Library Too

…really important for someone working on their own who needs to check things out, or just bounce a few ideas around.

- Quentin Colborn
Director, QC People Management Ltd

While you wait for a response from the Facebook group, you'll likely find answers in the resource-rich members' vault on our secure online portal as well.

It takes just 2 clicks and a quick keyword search using our Rapid Results Search Tool.

You'll instantly find precisely where your topic is covered in our extensive back catalogue of monthly magazines and audio seminars.

In under 30 seconds you can find exactly what you're after.

It's that quick and easy.

…And if you need a specific legal insight?

Then pose your question live to an expert employment lawyer in our monthly Q&A session.

It'll either be me or one of my prominent contemporaries. You'll get your answer immediately without having to pay any legal costs.

If you can't wait, you'll find where it's been answered before with a quick search of previous Q&A sessions.

Our clever index system means you can find a question, and in a single click get straight to the recorded answer.

But perhaps you need to dive deep and explore the different options open to you to solve a particularly tricky problem?

Then join one of our monthly HR Huddles. There you can run your specific situation past other HR professionals.

They'll offer their insights, share their experience and work WITH you to find a solution that works FOR you.

You'll find all of this in one convenient place - the HR Inner Circle.

It's Been A Labour Of Love Putting The HR Inner Circle Together So It Works For Professionals Like You

> It's great to see that we all experience tricky cases from time to time.
>
> - Annabelle Carey
> Managing Consultant, HR Services Partnership

I've spent years practising law and have become recognised as one of the UK's leading employment law barristers. I've even got my own radio show!

But more importantly for you, I've also developed another skill.

It's bringing useful employment expertise AND practical experience together in a way that supports busy, overworked (and sometimes stressed) HR professionals like you.

Everything you're likely to need is **literally at your fingertips**.

This will save you **time, energy** and **effort**.

Being a member also means your business and clients will see you as even MORE INFORMED about the intricacies of employment law.

They'll marvel at how well you keep up to date when you're busy working so hard for them.

You'll be seen making quicker decisions and implementing effective solutions to accelerate the growth of the organisation.

You'll make impressive time and cost savings for the business.

And those tricky, off-piste situations you've never come across before..?

Well, nothing will faze you, because you're backed up by an HR support system second to none.

But more importantly, you'll feel that pressure gently ease off.

With the relief you'll feel knowing that such great help and guidance is just a few minutes, you'll wonder how you survived without it!

That's Why I'm Inviting You To Join And Reap The Many Rewards Of Membership

► WWW.HRINNERCIRCLE.CO.UK ◄

Here's what you get when you join the HR Inner Circle:

Benefit #1- you'll get unlimited access to the hugely popular HR Inner Circle Facebook Private Group

- Tap into the vast wealth of knowledge, experience, insight and wisdom of the top 0.5% of your profession at any time, day or night.

- In less than 5 minutes you can post ANY HR question and get insightful answers and suggestions in a couple of hours or less, from some of the best in your profession.

- Fast track your impact by discovering effective shortcuts and workarounds from HR people who've been "there" and done "it".

- Expand and deepen your network of like minded individuals, secure in the knowledge they're as dedicated and as ambitious as you.

- Increase your prestige with your colleagues and stakeholders by being part of such an exclusive and prominent HR community.

- Gain confidence in your judgment and decisions by using the highly responsive community as a sounding board for your ideas.

Benefit #2 - you'll receive 11 copies of the HR Inner Circular Magazine every year

- Enjoy that satisfying "THUD" on your door mat every month when the postman delivers your very own copy of the HR Inner Circular magazine.

- Quickly discover exactly what the law says about key issues affecting HR professionals around the UK like you.

- Get concise and practical guidance on how employment law applies to the challenging situations and circumstances you deal with every day.

- Avoid the mistakes of others by applying the lessons from the in depth analysis of real life case studies.

- Benefit from a legal deep dive by the UK's leading employment law barrister into a topical employment question posed by a fellow member (perhaps you!).

- Review a summary of recent important Facebook Group discussions worthy of sharing, that you may have missed.

- Explore a range of related and relevant topics useful for your practice and your broader professional development.

Benefit #3 - Monthly Audio Seminars

- A 60 minute legal deep dive by me into an important subject relevant to you and your practice.

- Professionally recorded content recorded exclusively for the HR Inner Circle - you'll not find this information anywhere else.

- Carefully structured content that's easy to consume, understand and apply in your work as an HR professional.

- Episodes delivered every month so you can stay current on the latest issues affecting HR professionals.

- The convenience of listening to the recording online or downloading the mp3 for later enjoyment at a time suitable to your busy schedule (perfect for any commute).

Benefit #4 - you get an exclusive invite to a live online Q&A Session every fortnight, led by an expert employment lawyer

- Gain 60 minutes of live and direct access to the sharpest legal minds from my secret little black book of contacts.

- Get answers to your knottiest employment law questions, and solutions to your trickiest HR problems, from some of the brightest employment lawyers in the UK.

- Avoid having to pay the £300-£400 it would cost you to ask a lawyer your question outside of the HR Inner Circle.

- Benefit from valuable insights from the answers given to other members.

- If you can't attend live, watch the recording when it's convenient for you.

- Quickly access the recorded answer to any question asked in the session by simply clicking the question index for that session.

- Save time by downloading the session transcription to scan-read at a time suitable for you.

Benefit #5 - join a live Monthly Huddle with other HR Professionals to solve your most challenging HR problems

- Attend your very own mini-mastermind group of highly qualified, highly regarded and experienced fellow HR professionals to "group think" through an issue you're facing right now.

- Develop bespoke solutions to the unique problems and challenges you have to deal with in a safe, supportive and confidential environment.

- Feel safe knowing these online zoom calls are NOT recorded to respect the sensitivity of issues addressed and the privacy of those involved. [NOTE - a professional transcriber attends and takes written notes. An anonymised summary is then made available to the membership]

- Recent Huddle topics included changing employee benefits, mandatory vaccination, career breaks, sickness during disciplinaries, effective worker forums and hybrid working arrangements.

Benefit #6 - access our Templates & Resources Centre

- Gain immediate access to our library of the most popular and frequently used forms, assessments, agreements, checklists, letter templates, questionnaires and reports to help the busiest HR professionals save time and get things done quicker and easier.

- Download them as Word documents, so you can edit and personalise them to fit your business needs

- New templates added every single month

Benefit #7 - build your own Employment Law Library

- We send you several brand-new books on employment law several times each year

- Acquire your own physical library of concise, easy-to-read and fully updated textbooks

- Recent titles include Hiring Staff, Managing Sickness Absence, Spotting Malingering and Resolving Grievances

Benefit #8 - free Ticket to our Annual Conference

- The perfect opportunity to extend your personal network of fellow HR professionals.

- Meet up face to face with the people who've been supporting you in the Facebook Group and HR Huddles so you can deepen those connections even further.

- Gather key insights and takeaways to help you personally and professionally from some of the best speakers on the circuit. Previous speakers have covered motivation, dealing with difficult people, goal setting and productivity, decision making and social media marketing.

- Get instant access to recordings of all previous conferences so even if you can't attend in person, you can benefit from the event in your own time.

- Includes probably the best conference lunch you'll ever have - a bold claim I know, but we use outstanding caterers.

> **It never ceases to amaze me the amount of time and effort people put into the Facebook group, sharing their experiences, advice, and sage words of wisdom.**
>
> **- Emma Lister**
> HR Consultant, SME HR Services

Benefit #9 - your Personal Concierge will help you get the best out of your membership

- You get personal access to Nina who'll point you in the direction of exactly where to find what you need. She's supported hundreds of members over the 5 years she's been part of the team.

- Nina also works closely with the 11 back office staff that support the operation. In the extremely unlikely event she doesn't know where something is, she knows who will.

HOW MUCH DOES JOINING THE HR INNER CIRCLE COST?

There's no doubt in my mind the annual value of membership benefits is in the many thousands of pounds range.

But you're not going to pay anywhere near that.

Let me remind you of what that small monthly fee gives you every year

Access to the private Facebook Group	INCLUDED
HR Inner Circular Magazine subscription	INCLUDED
Monthly Audio Seminars	INCLUDED
Live Q&A sessions	INCLUDED
Monthly HR Huddles	INCLUDED
Templates & Resources Centre	INCLUDED
Employment Law Library	INCLUDED
Free ticket to the HR Inner Circle Annual Conference	INCLUDED
Your Personal Membership Concierge	INCLUDED

TOTAL PRICELESS

Another way of looking at your investment is this:

Because access to what you need is so quick…

Join today and that price is fixed for as long as you remain a member. You'll always pay the same, even if we increase the price to new members (which we regularly do).

…it's like having your very own part time, legally trained, assistant HR Business Partner, just waiting to provide you with all the answers you need…

▶ WWW.HRINNERCIRCLE.CO.UK ◀

Plus, With Membership Of The HR Inner Circle, You'll Also Get These 4 Additional Resources For FREE!

Additional Resource #1 - Handling Awkward Conversations

A video case study masterclass you can share with managers to train them to handle awkward staff disciplinary, performance and attitude problems. A huge time saver for you.

Additional Resource #2 - 6 x HR Employment Online Courses

Immediate, on demand access to six thorough, online HR courses (with more constantly added), including Employment Tribunal Compensation, Chat GPT for HR Professionals, Deconstructing TUPE, Changing Terms & Conditions, Unconscious Bias At Work and Handling Grievances.

Additional Resource #3 - Free listing on the Register of Investigators

Advertise your professional investigations service in our member's portal.

Additional Resource #4 - Significant discounts on sets of policies, contracts, and other courses.

Get member discounts on my Getting Redundancy Right and HR Policies products as well as other price reductions as new products are released.

▶ WWW.HRINNERCIRCLE.CO.UK ◀

I'm So Confident Joining The HR Inner Circle Is The Right Decision For You, Here's My

NO LIMITS

GUARANTEE

Take action and join the HR Inner Circle **now**.

If you're not 100% satisfied with your investment, you can cancel at ANY time.

Just tell us, and your membership will end immediately. No long-term contracts. No notice periods. No fuss.

I'm comfortable doing this because I know once you join, you'll find the support, the information and the strategies so useful, you'll never want to leave.

Before you decide though, let me be very clear about membership of the HR Inner Circle.

It's only for ambitious and dedicated HR professionals who want to accelerate and increase their impact by plugging into an HR ecosystem with its finger firmly on the pulse of what's working right now in HR.

If you're just plodding along and are content with just getting by, then this is probably not for you.

But if you're drawn to benefiting from standing shoulder to shoulder with some of the giants in the HR community who will help you solve your toughest problems, then joining the HR Inner Circle is the RIGHT decision for you.

Join here now:

▶ WWW.HRINNERCIRCLE.CO.UK ◀

JOIN TODAY

Daniel Barnett

P.S. Remember when you join you get unrestricted access to the private Facebook group, the monthly magazine delivered direct to your door, the monthly audio seminar, regular free books, templates, checklists and resources, on-demand video courses, over 100 audio seminars and back copies of magazines, live interactive Q&A sessions with a lawyer, focused monthly huddles with other HR professionals, a free ticket to the annual conference, your personal concierge plus a bunch of additional resources...